BRACKETEERING

BRACKETEERING

The Layman's Guide
to Picking the Madness in March

Andrew Clark

acta
PUBLICATIONS

BRACKETEERING
The Layman's Guide to Picking the Madness in March
by Andrew Clark

Edited by Gregory F. Augustine Pierce
Cover design by Tom A. Wright
Cover photo from BigStockPhoto.com. Used with permission.
Author photo by Jessica Gagnon
Text design and typesetting by Patricia A. Lynch

Published by ACTA Sports, a division of ACTA Publications, 4848 N. Clark Street, Chicago, IL 60077 (800) 397-2282 www.actapublications.com

Library of Congress Number: 2010938805
ISBN: 978-0-87946-446-2
Printed in the United States of America by Total Printing Systems
Year: 15 14 13 12 10
Printing: 5 4 3 2 First

CONTENTS

To my family,
the four most important people in my life.

And to Bill James,
who has been an unbracketable inspiration.

A NOTE TO THE READER

Bracketeering is meant to be a step-by-step, how-to guide that aids people in creating the most intelligent college basketball brackets possible. For the past six years I have utilized this system, tinkering and adding to it year after year. And now I feel I've perfected the ideals of my system enough to share them in very layman's terms. All I can say is that I hope (and I want to say that I'm sure) the rules contained herein will help you come tournament time.

That is the idea. The real fun of doing the brackets is in filling them out yourself, not in copying someone else's. So this book is aimed at helping you fill out *your own* brackets.

If, however, you *really* want to see my picks before you finish making your own, go to www.BRACKETEERINGthebook.com and sign up to be on our email list. I will send everyone on that list a copy of my picks at noon on the day before the field of 64 begins play. I'll also post my own "sheet of integrity" there just before the tip-off of the first game.

Of course, if we all do our Bracketeering perfectly, we'll have exactly the same picks all the way through the tournament. Well, maybe in an ideal world. But like I say, what would be the fun in that?

INTRODUCTION
And the Madness Begins

Ah, March Madness. It's that wonderfully enigmatic three-week stretch when I cheer for schools I've never heard of and root against those that rejected me when I was a high school senior. At this time of year, my living room becomes a makeshift bunker replete with Coke, pizza, junk food, and antacids. Each day of the tournament, I monopolize the family television and obsessively check my bracket, treating each contest as if it is the Super Bowl—even if it's just Texas A&M against Drexel. However, I'm not alone. Every year millions of people suddenly take an interest in college basketball for these three magical weeks. Some, like me, schedule our day around the tournament; others watch a few games here or there. But whether someone's interest is diehard or fleeting, there is no denying the tournament's popularity. Countless minutes are spent pouring over empty brackets in attempts to win office or family pools or those impossible $1,000,000 prizes from online competitions. Some will use their instincts to make selections, while others will make picks based on the academic strength of the schools involved. There are even those that will fill out their brackets using a blindfold. Seldom do these methods ever work.

But what if I told you there was a science to the NCAA tournament, a very attainable blend of logic and simple math to take the madness away from your March? I was once part of the masses, making my picks in a style that combined quick glances at season records and Ouija-board-like choices. What was the result? Years of busted brackets that picked Gonzaga to win the national title. (They never did, in case you're wondering.) My methods were even more reckless when you considered my interest in statistics, particularly sports statistics. During those days, I was a member of SABR (the Society for American Baseball Research), an organization which devotes itself to in-depth statistical baseball analysis. After years of failing brackets, I finally decided to try applying statistics and common-sense logic to my picks. I started by pinpointing three or four statistical categories that I thought were important and began analyzing how teams performed in these areas. Eventually, I created a few statistics of my own. That was six years ago. That was also the first time that I picked the champion correctly. And believe it or not, it was not Gonzaga.

For the past six years, I have been building on my original system, tinkering with it as I decided what is and isn't crucial when making picks for the NCAA Men's Basketball Tournament in March. Out of those six years, I have picked the national title winner on four occasions, using only one "sheet of integrity," as Mike Greenberg and Mike Golic of ESPN radio have dubbed it.

Now it's time to share this system—which I so cleverly call Bracketeering—with you. So where do we begin? Well, first, before launching into my round-by-round advice, it's important to lay the groundwork and give you my Golden Rule: *You must always plan ahead. Always.* Remember, in most bracket competitions, each contest is worth a certain amount of points per round. First-round games are usually worth only 1 or 10 points a piece, while picking the national champion is worth 32 or 320.[1]

With the first round, it is important to put yourself in a strong position, point-wise, going into round two, but you should also be wary of eliminating teams that have the potential to go far—or of falling in love with a team that is susceptible to getting bounced early—since that is how most brackets get busted. It's also easy to get discouraged after a nondescript first-round performance. Don't be. It isn't easy to post 28-4 or even 25-7 records after the first two days of the tournament. But if you don't, do not worry. You're not out of it yet. Like I said, the most important thing is that all of your championship-contending picks stay alive.

Final question before we begin: With the innumerable "experts" out there, why should you listen to me? Well, like I said, in the past six years, I've predicted the winner four times and have seen a fair amount of success with my bracket come tourney time. *Bracketeering* contains a lot of math—much of which you don't want to know—so what I am trying to do in this book is both create a set of simple rules for each round to help even the most casual of basketball fans pick their brackets, while also explaining the statistics that need to be utilized in order to make those picks. This way you don't need to be a Fields Medal[2] winner to beat out the people in your office pool. Also, if you do want to go a little deeper into the simple math involved, I'll let you know where to find that information and how

---

[1] They are basically the same point systems, with or without a zero at the end of the points. I'll use the 10/320 point system here. There are oddball contests that treat every game equally or weigh the results of each round differently, but you should ignore those, as I plan to do here. *Bracketeering* is aimed at the traditional, 64-slot brackets that are used in most Madness brackets on the Internet, in office and family pools, and in Las Vegas.

[2] For all of you non-nerds out there, this is the equivalent of the Noble Prize in mathematics—if they had one.

to go about using it effectively. Lastly, I should say that this system is not an all-out guarantee to the perfect bracket. Rather, Bracketeering gives you a much higher chance of making successful picks in contrast to some irrational system. I know a casual fan who makes her choices based on the strength of a school's law program. But Cornell can't play Duke in the title game every year.

So without further ado, let's begin. And let's have that fun we talked about.

Andrew Clark
Boston, Massachusetts

ROUND ONE
Getting Through Those First Two Days

Out of any level in the tournament, the first round contains the least amount of in-depth statistical analysis, as most picks can be made by utilizing a few simple, common-sense rules. Certainly some analysis needs to take place, and if you're struggling with your picks I definitely recommend using many of the rules I will introduce in later rounds. But thankfully, the first round—as exciting as it is—is rather straightforward in terms of making picks.

Before we dive into things, you need to know where to get all of these statistics that you're going to hear about. The first place I go to when the brackets are announced is the basketball statistics page for the NCAA (ncaa.com/statistics/m-baskbl-stats.html). Go to the current year of "Team and Player National Ranking Summary" and click on the most recently updated statistics. By clicking on any team, you can get both a team's ranking and performance in roughly 20 statistical categories. Also, for further information that's referenced in this book but is not located on NCAA.com, go to the NCAA statistics page on ESPN.com or visit a team's official website. With that said, let's get started.

Rule 1.1: Never, ever, ever pick a 16 seed over a 1 seed. Ever.

I should probably add another *ever* in there for good measure. There are very few reasons you can justify picking a 16 seed over a top seed. In fact, I can only think of three: 1) You went to a 16th-seeded school; 2) Your wife or girlfriend or husband or boyfriend went to a 16th-seeded school; or 3) Every single person on a top-seeded team has unexpectedly come down with some form of the norovirus. In the men's tournament, a 16 seed has never won even the opening game, so just based on history alone it is always a safe bet to pick the top seed.

Rule 1.2: Never pick a 15 seed over a 2 seed.

This pretty much follows the exact same logic from Rule 1.1, except that there have been four instances since the tournament expanded to 64 teams that a 15 seed has won in the opening round. Still, there is usually a reason why one team earns a 2 seed and another earns a 15 seed.

Rule 1.3: When it comes to the 14 seed against the 3 seed or the 13 seed against the 4 seed, you can now start looking for an upset. But remember the Golden Rule.

Picking the 14 or the 13 is a risk, and if you are going to do so, proceed with caution. First of all, don't pick a 14 seed to upset a 3 seed that has the chance to win the championship. You could be sacrificing 320 points for a measly 10. So, if you are going to make this choice, at least make sure that the 3 seed or the 4 seed you are picking to lose is tragically flawed and doomed to lose in the first few rounds.

Also, make sure that the 14 seed or 13 seed you are picking is a stud. Actually, that's a great segue to our next rule.

Rule 1.4: If you want the smartest upset pick, look for the most balanced Cinderella team that is playing a flawed top seed.

How do you find out which teams are balanced and which teams aren't? It's a lot easier than it sounds, actually. Without getting too deep into the statistical side of things, the most likely upset will happen when a low-seeded team that doesn't turn the ball over has a positive rebound margin, shoots the ball well, and has at least a +5 point-scoring margin (amongst other things) squares off against a high seed that has an average or below-average showing in all of those areas. In fact, I have the perfect anecdote for this.

When it came time to fill out my 2010 bracket, I fell in love with a team I had never heard of before: Murray State. Even though they were a 13 seed from the Ohio Valley Conference, Murray State was a team with a dominant scoring margin (+17, 3rd in the country), an impressive rebound margin (+6, 18th overall), and strong showings in a number of other statistics. To make things even better, the Racers[3] were playing a flawed Vanderbilt squad that, despite a respectable scoring margin, had rather average numbers in respect to rebounds and turnovers—not to mention a penchant for committing personal fouls. Because I felt Vanderbilt wouldn't go far in the tournament, and I absolutely loved everything about Murray State, I decided to make the "gamble" and go with the Racers. The result? Murray State beat Vanderbilt, 66-65.

---

[3] To date, I'm not exactly sure what a Murray State Racer actually is.

Rule 1.5: Make sure that no key injuries have occurred on teams that you think may go far.

This rule should go without saying, but you must do a quick background check on all of your major contenders to make sure that no important player has gone down with a broken leg or a case of dysentery. It can cripple an entire bracket. I'm not saying you have to be so thorough that you check the lifetime health records of every player on every team (knowing that the backup power forward for Cornell had mono when he was in eighth grade won't help you out very much). But try to keep abreast of any key injuries that would significantly weaken a team. For example, three weeks before the 2010 tournament, Purdue's star forward Robbie Hummel tore his ACL, a part of your body that you need for things such as playing basketball. Without Hummel, the 4th-seeded Boilermakers were a completely different team and got blown out by Duke in the Sweet Sixteen, despite their 26-4 regular season record. Making that quick check for injuries can really make a difference, and there are all kinds of websites that publish that info after the field for the tournament has been announced. Try ESPN.com and SI.com, for example.

Rule 1.6: Beware of the 5 seed against the 12 seed matchup. And while you're at it, watch out for the 6 against the 11.

Historically, it's these two matchups that produce the highest number of "upsets." Since the tournament began its 64-team format in 1985, the 5 and 6 seeds have won their first-round games roughly two-thirds of the time, which means the underdog has won one-third of the time. Upsets can happen anywhere in the tournament, but they seem to happen most often with these two matchups.

To spot the best upsets, remember Rule 1.4. And never forget that Golden Rule. In 2010, 5th-seeded Butler made it all the way to the title game, so you wouldn't have wanted to pick 12th-seeded UTEP over them.

Rule 1.7: Scoring margin is the most important statistic available, even more than a team's record.

Out of every statistic available to you, nothing—and I mean *nothing*—is more important than scoring margin. Scoring margin is the difference between how many points a team scores per game and how many points it gives up. It is the ultimate measure of how strong any team is. There can be teams that have incredible offensive outputs who can't stop other teams from scoring, which ultimately makes them useless in a tournament filled with strong, balanced teams. A prime example of this was the 2010 Providence College squad, a non-tournament team that was 3rd in the country in scoring offense with an eye-popping 82.4 PPG. However, the Friars were 333rd in the nation in scoring defense, allowing an equally eye-popping 82.2 OPPG. Ultimately, this meant that the Friars had no advantage whatsoever.

The higher a team's positive scoring margin, the more balanced they are on both sides of the ball. How important is scoring margin? Well, consider the 2008 NCAA title game, which featured Kansas (number one in the nation in scoring margin that year) against Memphis (number two in scoring margin that year). If you had just made out your brackets that year using only that single statistic, you would have won a lot of office and family pools. There are obviously many other statistics at play when considering individual matchups, but of any metric easily available to the average fan nothing is more revealing about a team than scoring margin.

Rule 1.8: When it comes to the close matchups (7 versus 10, 8 versus 9), try to look for stark statistical differences. Don't try to make close calls using team records or a program's pedigree. Seldom will that work.

Traditionally the 7/10 and 8/9 matchups are the hardest to choose. These are teams that are typically similar in terms of strength, which is why you need to look for some advantage between teams amongst the key statistics: scoring margin, created-possession margin (see Round 3), and shooting percentages—which are the "big three" statistics that you should be using to evaluate teams. If teams are really, really close in all of those statistics, then you can begin to use secondary statistical tie-breakers (we will get more into additional statistics that can be used to evaluate close matchups when we look at the later rounds in the tournament). And if even those stats do not give one team the edge over the other, then we can get into last–ditch, third-tier tiebreakers, such as the strength of each team's competition that year (the SEC is always tougher than the MAC), how old and experienced a team is (juniors and seniors are usually better in tournaments than freshmen, unless the freshmen are named Derrick or Carmelo), and coaching (chances are that a squad led by Coach K or Roy Williams or Bill Self will have a tiny edge over a rookie head coach, even if both teams are dead-even every other way).

Rule 1.9: It should go without saying, but don't let biases or hunches alter your picks. Stick with the Bracketeering system.

This may seem like chiding, but every year people will make picks due to their strong hatred of or preference for certain teams based on things that happened in previous years.[4]

When I was younger, I had a tendency to put Gonzaga in my Final Four every year. Part of it was their mascot; part of it was their fun style of basketball; part of it was that I was hypnotized by Dick Dickau's floppy bangs. But the point is, it always killed my bracket, because my favorite team was usually primed to lose early. Now that I'm older—and, I like to think, wiser—I make my picks based on logic and numbers. I'm proud to say that Gonzaga hasn't been in my Final Four in the past five years, as tempting as it's been to pick them. And believe me, it has been very tempting to pick them.

---

[4] Remember, in college basketball, as opposed to the pros, what a team was like last year—much less four years ago—is not relevant. Kids leave college all the time, and the better the player the sooner they tend to leave.

Down to the Final Fou—Eh, Thirty-Two

So it might seem that congratulations are in order. You've picked 32 games and the hard part must be over, right? Not so fast. From here on out, everything is an uphill climb, getting more and more difficult round after round. But not to worry. Though you'll need to put a bit of work in from now on, you'll be introduced to a series of very uncomplicated statistics and simple rules that will allow you to finish up your bracket before your boss catches you.

Rule 2.1: All teams are now vulnerable. Even 1 and 2 seeds.

Often people will make the mistake of picking top seeds to go deep into the tournament just because they are top seeds. Their logic: Because a team is a top seed, they must be the best, right? Well, not so fast. Though you should never pick a 1 or a 2 seed to lose in the first round, you need to look closely at the matchups that these "top teams" face in the second round. Certainly there is some reason that a team earned top billing, but be wary of advancing squads just because of these high seedings. A recent example? Look at Villanova, a 2 seed in the 2010 tournament. People got caught up with the Wildcats' 24-7 record, the dominance of their all-world guard Scottie Reynolds, their stiff competition in the Big East, and their top-ten national ranking. However, these flashy numbers clouded some troubling red flags—such as the fact that Villanova ranked 278th in the nation in scoring defense and had terrible issues with personal fouls (we will get into the impact of the foul line in a bit). When I filled out my "sheet of integrity" in 2010, I immediately put an asterisk next to Villanova, especially because their likely second-round matchup was with a phenomenal St. Mary's squad that was strong across the board in almost every important statistic. Not surprisingly, St. Mary's— a relatively unknown 10 seed—took out the overhyped Wildcats. Even the tournament's top overall seed, Kansas, lost last year after having the unfortunate draw of playing a dangerous 9th-seeded Northern Iowa team that had one of the nation's most dominating defenses. The lesson here? Don't be so fast to pencil in top seeds to win their second-round games. I'm not saying always go with the underdog, but definitely keep a watchful eye—though it's usually easy to scope out the "upsets."

Rule 2.2: In the grand scheme of things, statistics are more important than team records. In fact, don't even look at a team's record when making your picks.

Ultimately, records are a rather misleading measure of a team. Certainly if a team is undefeated or winless—or has an impressively high winning percentage in one of the more difficult conferences in the nation—then there is some clout to their record. But what I'm mainly concerned about is people who get wrapped up in teams that post 30-3 marks in talentless conferences or those who red-flag teams with double-digit losses that play stiff competition. When it comes tournament time, regular season records don't really matter at all. A potentially dangerous team may have suffered a regular-season injury which caused a string of losses. Another contender may have lost a collection of close one or two-point games against tough competition that skewed its record a bit. And a faux contender may have cruised to a 25-7 mark while playing against junior-high caliber squads.

Let's do a case study to illuminate this point, using the greatest example of a misleading record within the last ten years: the 2001-2002 Indiana University Hoosiers. During the season, the Hoosiers had an inauspicious 20-11 record, which led to a 5 seed in the tournament. Yet despite this record, Indiana made it all the way to the championship game. Why? Indiana's record doesn't tell you that seven of those losses were by six or fewer points, meaning their record could have easily been 27-4 if the tides had turned a little differently. Further, Indiana's nondescript record failed to reflect its strengths, including an impressive defense and an overall fairly well-balanced team that definitely had the potential to make a long run in the tournament. In conclusion, to make my favorite law school professor proud, think of a team's record as evidence that is unfairly prejudicial. It really doesn't prove much about a team, but it's a number that many people can take too seriously and let cloud their judgment. In this courtroom, the Honorable Judge Bracketeering is not allowing a team's record in. Motion dismissed.

Rule 2.3: They may not seem to be a big deal, but guess what? Fouls are the silent killer. Avoid picking teams that have issues with fouling.

When you're watching a basketball game, fouls just seem to be part of the game—and a very annoying part to boot. But in basketball—particularly college basketball—fouls can make the difference between a win and a loss. In the college game, after a team commits its seventh foul of the half, their opponent goes to the line and shoots what is called a "one-and-one." That means they get to shoot one free throw, and if they make it, they get to shoot another. After a team commits ten fouls in a half, their opponent gets two shots no matter what. Simple, right? Well, when it comes to games that pit evenly talented squads against one another, fouls oftentimes make the difference. Teams that have a propensity to constantly foul throughout the course of a game are basically giving their opponent the chance to accumulate free, uncontested points. And there are those teams that have a tendency to foul more than others. To illuminate the critical importance of fouls, I'd like to do a case study, but before I do that, it seems apropos to introduce the next rule, which pretty much walks hand-in-hand with this one.

Rule 2.4: When teams that struggle with the fouling bug play squads that thrive from the free throw line, disaster typically ensues—for the former, of course. As much as you should avoid picking teams that struggle with fouling, absolutely try to avoid them in these situations.

This rule may seem to go without saying, and it may seem boring. But it's absolutely crucial. If a team that has a tendency to foul (look for squads with 18 or more fouls per game) is matched up against a team that shoots a high percentage from the free-throw line (72 percent or better), then the high-fouling team is going to be at a disadvantage. And obviously, the higher the fouls and the higher the opposing free-throw percentage, the more damning this disadvantage will be. Trust me, there is a crippling and game-changing handicap that occurs.

I mentioned it briefly earlier, but the most effective example I can think of to illuminate this point is the second-round matchup between "high-powered" Villanova and St. Mary's in the 2010 tournament.

Going into the tournament, St. Mary's had the 5th-best free-throw-shooting percentage in the entire country, as the Gaels shot at an impressive 76.4 percent clip from the charity stripe. On the other end of things, Villanova entered the tournament ranked 327th in the country in fouls committed per game, averaging 22.4 per contest, an absolutely dismal, dismal number. Did I mention that is dismal? Here's a question for you. What do you think happened when one of the most foul-happy teams in the country played one of the best free-throw shooting teams? Things did not end well for the Wildcats, and Villanova lost the game, 75-68. Fouls were the reason, of course. The Wildcats fouled the Gaels 18 times, slightly below their season average. However, St. Mary's attempted a total of 26 foul shots and, consistent with their impressive season average, they shot 76.9 percent from the line, going 20-for-26 on the day. Even though Villanova themselves went 11-for-11 from the line (they were also a great foul-shooting team), St. Mary's didn't have the kinds of fouling problems the Wildcats did. And so it goes, as the late Kurt Vonnegut would say.

Also, if you have the time and want to go a little bit deeper into things, you can compare a team's propensity to foul against their opponent's ability to get to the line. As much as teams struggle with fouls, there are those squads that have a distinct ability to get to the free-throw line. It is kind of an art form, actually. In 2010, 2nd-seeded Kansas State averaged an incredible 30.5 free throws each game throughout the season. That's a really difficult statistic to wrap one's mind around, and for the Wildcats, it created an advantage. Even though they weren't the most prolific team from the charity stripe, shooting a rather dull 66.5 percent, the Wildcats led the nation by sinking just over 20 free throws a night. Getting to the line is a skill that's hard to teach, so having a team that makes their living off the easiest shot on the floor is nothing to ignore. On that note, let's look at the final rule for the second round.

Rule 2.5: Be wary of teams that rely on the three-point shot for a high percentage of their offense, especially when they play squads who shut down outside perimeter shooting. Those teams prove to be risky picks that can get eliminated very quickly.

It's easy to get caught up in the glitz and glamour of the three-pointer, and it's hard to deny that an effective three-point shot can be a potent weapon. Also, it's absolutely mesmerizing to watch a team drain shots from 25 feet away, shooting with such precision that the ball doesn't even appear to graze the net. But it is imperative to observe how much of a team's offense comes from the three-pointer. If a team relies on the three-pointer for a third or more of their offense, one off-night in the tournament can be a quick ticket home. And if a team relies on the three-pointer, they are especially vulnerable if they are playing a squad that defends the perimeter well and shuts down outside shooters. If a team that lives and dies by the three plays a team that effectively defends the three-ball, the squad that shoots from downtown will die more times than not.

Hmm, I smell an example coming up. The most helpful illustration of this three-point issue is shown in the 2010 first-round game between Xavier and Minnesota, two at-large bids in the tournament. During its regular season, Minnesota relied pretty heavily on the three, as 21 points each game came from beyond the arc, a slightly higher number, on average, than most teams. Roughly 29 percent of Minnesota's offense came from beyond the arc (compared to Michigan State, a Final Four team, at 19.8 percent). Certainly there were teams that year that relied on the three-pointer even more than Minnesota, but it's undeniable that the shot was pivotal for the Golden Gophers. And unfortunately for Minnesota, their first-round opponent was well-trained in the art of stopping the three-point shot, as the Xavier Musketeers held teams to a stingy 29.4 percent success rate from beyond the arc. When these two teams squared off, Minnesota managed to make its requisite seven three-pointers. But it took the Gophers 26 attempts to get there, as they shot a dismal 26.9 percent from downtown. Three-point misses can lead to all sorts of trouble—especially when there's an abundance of them—from disproportionate rebound margins (which we will explore in a bit) to changes in momentum. So keeping track of this rule is very important, particularly in the early rounds, where some funny things can happen. Also, as you probably already know or can guess: Xavier won, 65-54.

ROUND THREE
Making the Sweet Sixteen a Bit Sweeter

In the previous round, I introduced a few simple, obvious, ubiquitous statistics that you need to keep in mind when making your picks.

In this round, you'll learn one of the most important statistics in the game of basketball—one they don't talk about on TV or in the newspapers—that should be used in every round where there is no absolutely obvious pick.

Also, there is another thing that I should mention. All of the rules and statistics that are being discussed in these later rounds can and should be used in each round. Just because I talk about something in round three, for example, doesn't mean that you shouldn't use it to help you make a close choice in round one.

And those ground rules you learned about in round one are meant to help you in subsequent rounds—well, at least the ones that still apply.

Rule 3.1: Okay, from here on out, seedings don't matter. Don't even look at that little parenthetical number next to a team's name. Whether a team is a (1) or a (12) doesn't matter anymore.

How can this be? Certainly if a team is a top seed and their opponent is a double-digit seed, the top seed has an automatic advantage, right? Wrong. Seedings are misleading at this stage in the tournament. Case in point—and this is something that many of you probably remember—the 2006 George Mason Patriots. Ah, the Patriots. Before the tournament, they were an afterthought. As an 11 seed that played in the Colonial Athletic Association, George Mason had been written off on most brackets by the first or second game of the tournament. But this 11 seed wound up in the Final Four before losing to eventual champion Florida. How could this happen? Weren't they an 11 seed? It can happen and did happen because George Mason was a powerful team with one of the highest scoring margins and toughest defenses in the nation, something their double-digit seeding refused to acknowledge. A lot of brackets got busted that year, mine included.

There is a moral to this story for us Bracketeers: If a team has been good enough to win its first two games, it might just be good enough to win them all. It's too easy to write a team off just because they have a low seeding. If you thought they were good enough to make the Sweet Sixteen, then you still must, must, *must* look at their statistics against the other teams in the tournament as you make your picks going forward. The next George Mason could be lurking in the corner. Actually, let's hope no one is lurking in any corner. That sounds both creepy and dangerous and has no place in college basketball. The NBA? Well, maybe.

What exactly is a created-possession margin? I'm glad you asked. It is a formula I created when I was a nerdy high school junior to determine the margin by which teams "create" more possessions for themselves than the other team creates for themselves. Pretty obvious, no? Created-possession margin is determined by a very simple formula: (Rebound Margin) + (Turnover Margin) = Created-Possession Margin.

In simple English (it must be much more complicated in Urdu), created-possession margin is how many additional possessions a team will create for itself compared to its opponent by superior rebounding and/or by causing more or commiting fewer turnovers than their opponents do. It's common sense.

However, rather than expound on how important rebounds and turnovers are to the outcome of a game—and believe me, they are critical—I'm going to consolidate everything under the umbrella of this one statistic and ask you to trust me. It will help you win your brackets.

Why is created-possession margin so crucial? I want you to think about it in these terms: Each possession has the potential to be worth between one and three points, depending on how it is ultimately utilized. (Let's just ignore the extremely rare four-point play and the mythical five-pointer.) When a team has a significant amount of additional possessions when compared to its opponent, that team, in principle (and in reality, which is nice when both occur at once), has a chance for additional points. Looking at rebound margin and turnover margin on an individual basis is certainly important and helpful, but combining the two statistics into one measure really shows the overall advantage a team creates for itself.

Case studies are really the best way to illuminate this point. Let's take a look at the sixteen teams that made it to the third round of the 2010 NCAA Men's Basketball Tournament and where they had ranked amongst all tournament teams in created-possession margin at the end of the regular season:

Team	Rebound Margin	Turnover Margin	Created Possession Margin	Rank Among Tournament Teams
Duke	5.9	3.8	9.7	2
WVU	6.8	1.8	8.6	5
Michigan State	9.0	-1.1	7.9	8
Washington	4.3	3.3	7.6	10
Kansas St.	5.1	2.5	7.6	11
Kentucky	7.9	-0.4	7.5	12
Xavier	5.4	-0.1	5.3	19
Ohio State	2.1	2.9	5.0	23
Butler	3.7	1.3	5.0	24
Syracuse	3.7	1.2	4.9	25
Cornell	3.3	1.6	4.9	26
Baylor	6.7	-1.8	4.9	27
Northern Iowa	3.0	1.7	4.7	31
Purdue	-0.7	5.0	4.3	35
Tennessee	0.7	3.5	4.2	36
St. Mary's	4.4	-0.4	4.0	40

There's great value in combining the two measures together, which is demonstrated by Michigan State and Kentucky, who ranked 8th and 12th, respectively, among all tournament teams that year.

If someone was to simply glance at the turnover margin of those two teams, immediate questions would have to be raised. How can a team be primed to succeed if they turn the ball over more than their opponent? Where is the advantage? Granted, having a negative turnover margin is nothing to be proud of. But with both Kentucky and Michigan State, the possessions lost through turnovers were quickly made up through their superlative rebound margins.

There's another thing to note about the chart above: Roughly half of the teams (seven out of sixteen) that made it to the Sweet Sixteen that year were ranked amongst the top twenty teams in the tournament in created-possession margin. (It's also worth mentioning that the team which won the entire tournament, Duke University, sits at the top of the list.)

Obviously, if two teams with high created-possession margins play one another, the advantage might not be profound. But if you have a squad like Duke playing against Purdue, which occurred in the Sweet Sixteen in 2010, the effect can change a game. Duke entered the tournament with a dominant +9.7 created-possession margin, while Purdue was amongst the bottom half of the tournament field in that department with a modest +4.3 margin. What happened when these two worlds collided? Despite losing the battle on the turnover side, Duke managed to create 16 more possessions than Purdue through shear dominance on the boards. This kind of monopoly creates a stark advantage, whether Duke was using the ball to create points or simply keeping the ball out of Purdue's hands. Duke won, by the way, 70-57. No surprise there.

Ultimately, when it comes to created-possession margin, look for teams that have a margin of five or higher, as five is really the benchmark for a meaningful advantage. The higher a margin is, of course, the greater the advantage. It might even be exponential. When teams like Duke have margins near or above ten, this statistic becomes a number that puts the entire rest of the tournament field at an instant disadvantage.

A team's created possession margin is not the end-all, be-all statistic. Otherwise, this would be a very short book. In fact, think about it: What type of an advantage is a created-possession margin if a team can't score? Not-so-coincidentally, that leads us to our next rule.

Rule 3.3: Possessions are useless if a team doesn't use them effectively. Make sure the teams you pick are efficient with the basketball.

This is a simple little rule that has a major impact on brackets. A team can have all the possessions in the world, but if they can't score, what's the point? Make sure that the teams you pick can score. A transitory glance at a team's shooting percentages can go a long way. To establish a quick set of benchmarks: In order to display an efficient offense, a team must have a field-goal percentage of roughly 45 percent or better; a three-point percentage of 36 percent or better; and from the free-throw line at least—*at least*—a 70 percent shooting mark.

What kind of an impact can a disparity in shooting percentages cause? Let's use a quick little example—a rather extreme example, to say the least. In the 2010 tournament, Kentucky created seven more possessions than its Sweet Sixteen opponent West Virginia. However, the Wildcats lost 73-66, even though West Virginia had an off-day and shot 38.5 percent from the field. The problem was that Kentucky failed to efficiently execute their offense. How bad was it? The Wildcats fired a reprehensible 32 shots from beyond the three-point line, making just four on the day for a paltry 12.5 percent mark. It's also worth mentioning that Kentucky shot just 55.2 percent from the free-throw line. This is an example of a catastrophically inefficient offense in action (and these numbers were below Kentucky's season averages), but it's meant to illustrate a point. If you're going to pick a team at this point in your bracket—and especially if your decision is weighed heavily upon a high created-posession margin—make sure that the team you're picking utilizes their possessions efficiently. Glance over their field-goal, three-point, and free-throw percentages, and—as advised in the previous round—be wary of teams that rely on the three-point shot and kind to those that earn their points at the foul line.

Rule 3.4: When evaluating a team's statistics, the numbers must be adjusted against an opponent's averages before they can be fully considered. Such an adjustment gives you a much clearer idea of how much of an advantage a team will have.

There's a fairly simple logic behind the final rule for this round. A team's numbers may be great and impressive and, without even looking at their opponent, you can pretty much tell that they should wipe the floor with whomever steps in against them. But that's not exactly true. Before you can tell how much of an impact a team's prowess in a certain statistic will be, you must compare that statistic against its opponent's performance in that category. This rule is imperative with shooting percentages (field-goal and three-point—not foul shooting, obviously) and is also useful when comparing possession creation.

For the purpose of illustrating this rule, let's focus on shooting percentage. In 2010, the 10th-seeded St. Mary's Gaels—(who would be a top-three seed if seedings were given based on nicknames) came into the tournament with rather auspcious shooting percentages, ranking 11th in the nation in field-goal percentage

(48.7 percent from the floor) and fourth in three-point percentage (41.2 percent). Now granted, there was a mild inflation in St. Mary's numbers coming from the WCC— a mild, not drastic inflation— which is something we will explore shortly. But it's hard to ignore numbers that strong. Unfortunately for the Gaels—who managed first and second-round victories over Richmond and Villanova, respectively—the Baylor Bears were their Sweet Sixteen foe. And the Bears were defensive stalwarts on the floor, holding opponents to a 38.4 percent shooting-percentage from the floor (9th in the country). As you can imagine, the Gaels did not manage their usual 48.7 percent night against Baylor. No. In fact, St. Mary's managed to make just 35.2 percent of their shots and shot at a paltry 27.3 percent clip from beyond the arc. That's not going to win a basketball game in the NCAA tournament's third round.

Another example of an adjustment is to quickly calculate the average between a team's field-goal percentage and their opponent's defensive field-goal percentage. Obviously, the actual game result won't always be exactly what this new adjusted number hints that it should be, but calibrating these percentages gives you a better idea of how impactful a team's statistics really are. And you can do the same thing with created possesions by comparing one team's margin against their opponent. For instance, when Duke (+9.7 created-possession margin) met Baylor (+4.9) in 2010, the difference between the two showed that Duke should still have an advantage, in this case +4.8. When they played the actual game, the Blue Devils ended up creating six more possessions than the Bears. Like I mentioned above, such head-to-head adjustments will not tell you exactly how a game will go, but a quick recalibration of the numbers provides you with a more reasonable idea about how much of an impact a particular statistic will have.

How to Pick Four of Those Eight Elite Teams

Okay, now we are down to picking among the truly elite teams in the tournament, where the work gets a bit harder and it takes more than a few minutes. Fortunately, I still have some tricks left for making those tough calls. At this point, you have probably realized that only a small number of teams ever had what it takes to go all the way, and chances are that you have picked most of them if you have been following the Bracketeering method. So now let's focus on helping you make your final tough calls among some very good teams.

Rule 4.1: High block tallies can be the difference maker in a close game.

Compared to other metrics, such as created-possession margin, the effect of blocked shots tends to be much smaller on who wins games at this level. Yet even though the effect is smaller, blocks can still have an impact on the outcome of a close game. Let's think of blocks in a different light, shall we? In the box score, when a shot is blocked, it is counted as a missed shot. If ten shots are blocked, it counts as ten missed shots. Simple, right? Yes, it is. The problem is that not many people understand this. Think of a block as a hands-on subtraction of between two and three *potential points*, that is, points that could have possibly been made by a team but weren't.

For teams that are poised to win by a blowout margin, blocks won't have *too* significant of an effect on the outcome of a contest. However, if you have a pair of teams that are relatively close to one another, or you're just having a difficult time committing to one team or another, then blocks can be a decisive tiebreaker. An important measure of how impactful blocks will be on the outcome of a game lies in block margin. That's right. Another margin statistic. Though not as important as scoring margin or created-possession margin, block margin—if drastic—can influence a game.

And here comes another case study. One of the most prolific blocking teams in recent memory, the 2008-2009 UConn Huskies, were heavily aided by their shot-swatting skills. (Try saying that three times fast.) The Huskies were dominant compared to their opponents, chiefly because of Hasheem Thabeet, their unmatchable seven-foot center from the basketball hotbed of Tanzania. They averaged 7.8 blocks per game compared to their opponents, who averaged 3.5 blocks per game (a margin of +4.3). That means that the Huskies were able to tangibly take away eight to twelve more potential points than their opponent each game. In the 2009 Elite Eight, the Huskies were matched up against Missouri, a very tough 3 seed out of the Big 12. In their matchup, which the Huskies won 82-75, UConn carried a block margin of +7, meaning that they tangibly took away between 14 and 21 potential points from the Tigers. This was a very interesting game, as UConn turned the ball over nearly 20 times but won the rebound battle—likely due to their plethora of blocks. So it is in situations like this that blocks can become a game-breaking statistic.

Rule 4.2: By this point, you need to make sure that the teams you pick going forward are well-balanced and have no discernible weaknesses that can easily get exposed. A glaring weakness tends to get a team bounced before the Final Four.

At this stage of the tournament—this critical stage where you are picking your Final Four teams—one of the key things that you must, *must* do is avoid picking teams that are not statistically balanced, unless they are overwhelmingly dominant in just about every other statistical category. What do I mean by finding teams that are statistically balanced? The teams you should be picking to be in your Final Four typically should not have any demonstrative weaknesses. These picks should have respectable scoring margins (though there should also be respectable offensive and defensive point averages), respectable created-possession margins, respectable shooting percentages (field-goal, three-point, and free-throw) and defensive-shooting percentages, and to a lesser extent, respectable block margins. The operative word here is *respectable*. I'm not saying that in order to be a winner, every team must have record-breaking stats in these areas, but obviously the more impressive showing in each statistic, the better. But it's so, so important that you don't have teams in your Final Four more tragically flawed than Achilles. It's pretty easy to spot these doomed squads. If you look quickly at the NCAA website—the one that lists a team and its performance and rankings in about twenty different statistics—you should immediately red flag teams that are not ranked within the top 150 teams in the nation (that's roughly the top 50 percent) in those important statistics we have talked about. And the lower a team ranks, the larger and redder that flag should get.

To make things a bit easier, here are a few examples of flawed squads some people had recklessly picked to go the distance in the

2010 tournament that were brought down pretty quickly by their glaring weakness. The first team to illustrate this was the top-seeded Syracuse Orangemen, who did impress in a number of statistical categories, as they had the top-ranked field-goal percentage in the country (51.6 percent), the 6th-ranked scoring margin (+14.6 points), and the 6th-ranked scoring offense (81.5 points per game). However, the Orangemen should have been Redflagged[5] immediately due to a few key statistical flaws, chiefly their 15.1 turnovers per game (272nd in the country) and less-than stellar 67.1 free-throw percentage (228th). The prowess of the Orangemen in those previously mentioned statistical categories was going to carry them a few rounds, but these flaws were too drastic not to eventually catch up with them. And guess what? In their Sweet-Sixteen matchup with Butler, Syracuse committed 18 turnovers compared to just 7 by Butler. By giving Butler this advantage, the Orangemen shot themselves in the metaphorical foot and ultimately lost 63-59. Another example I've harped on already is that tragically flawed 2010 Villanova squad, the one that ranked 327th in the nation on fouls per game and 278th in scoring defense. It's also worth mentioning that Villanova had a fairly average showing in a number of other categories as well, which all proved to be a perfect storm of predictable failure. The ultimate point is that you must make sure that you are not picking teams that are fatally flawed to advance to the far reaches of the tournament. Otherwise, you will just be violating that ever-so-Golden Rule.

---

[5] Nice play-on-words with the colors, no?

> **Rule 4.3:** As a way to help you break ties among your Elite Eight, keep in mind that a team's stats may be inflated based on what conference they play in. It's not a drastic inflation, but keep in mind that it exists. Let's just call it "Conference Factor."

This is not a measure that you should ever *rely* on to make a decision. However, it should be in the back of your mind when it comes to making really difficult decisions for late in the tournament. Conference Factor is exactly what it sounds like: a determination of how much playing in a certain conference affects a team's statistical performance. These kinds of measures have existed in all sorts of sports as a way of keeping statistical performances in perspective. (One of the first that comes to mind is called "Ballpark Factor," a statistic that is used in baseball to establish how much a certain ballpark inflates or deflates offensive numbers. By using Ballpark Factor, certain parks which are notorious for enhancing offensive performances, such as Coors Field in Colorado, are exposed for their impact on statistics.)

The problem with Conference Factor is that it changes year to year, so for the purposes of this book—rather than create some sort of long-winded, nerdy algorithm—we will evaluate the strength of a conference using a variety of methods. Traditionally, Conference Factor won't be that determinative of a tiebreaker in a game between two teams that play in those major conferences, like the Big East and SEC, where the competition is almost universally stiff. However, with teams from smaller conferences like the WAC, it's worth taking a look at the level of competition a team with dominant statistics faced in order to reach high levels of performance. This is not meant to completely take away the accomplishments of a team that has put up great numbers. Rather, it's meant to create a cognizance in more difficult decision-making situations that a team's numbers—if close to their opponent's—may not be as overwhelmingly impressive as you initially think.

So how is Conference Factor determined? A collection of methods can be used, depending on how much time you have. The quickest way is to look at the records of all the teams in the conference that the squad you're evaluating plays in. Another quick method is to look at a measure called RPI, which factors in winning percentage, opponent's winning percentage, and opponent's opponents' winning percentage. These RPI rankings can be found anywhere, from ESPN. com to SI.com, and it gives you a quick idea of a team's strength of schedule. The next step after that—and the one I recommend most if you have the time—is to look at the statistical performances of all the teams in a conference so that you have a true idea of what kinds of teams a certain squad faced. Like I said, if you're pressed on time, use the short methods of checking on win-loss records in a conference or RPI. But if you really want to get an in-depth look at the level of competition in a conference, analyze all the stats of each team in that conference. And remember, Conference Factor is not meant to be a go-to measure, but rather a last ditch effort to break ties. If you relied on Conference Factor instead of other far more important metrics, then teams like George Mason in 2006 would have been eliminated in the first round solely for being from a non-power conference. Remember, Conference Factor is simply meant to break ties in close situations by giving you an idea how heavily you should weigh other statistics you are analyzing. That's all.

Four Divided by Two

Les Quatres Finale[6]—or the Final Four, as it is called in America, the only country that actually has a nationwide college basketball tournament—is really the yardstick that most brackets are measured by. Sure it's fun to go 26-6 in the first round. But two weeks later, when you have zero teams left in the tournament, that first-round mark means nothing. Around offices, around schools, on the TV and the radio, the question is always "How many of the Final Four did you get right?" And when it comes to your bracket, these are heavily weighed games that either make you or break you, since they are usually worth 160 points a piece. Chances are, you love the four teams you have left. Now how do you pick just two of them?

You should continue Bracketeering, that is, use all the steps and measures that we have learned about up to this point. But when that's not good enough, and it's a bit too hard to pick one team over another, there are still a few more tricks and metrics left to break ties.

Also, how do you deal with multiple bracket entries instead of (or in addition to) your "sheet of integrity"? When it comes to round five, one of the most critical points of the tournament, more and more questions arise. Thankfully, the answers aren't too, too difficult to solve.

---

[6] Chances are, this is wrong. I never actually studied French.

Rule 5.1: When dealing with multiple bracket entries, follow the numbers and don't always try to spread out your picks or "cover you bet" (ahem, not that I condone using Bracketeering for gambling purposes).

Multiple entries are a common occurrence for most people who fill out a bracket come tournament time. There are those who enter their office pool, then will enter one or more with their friends, then with their friends' friends, then with their old college fraternity, and, if there's time, they might enter a family pool as well. I know people who have been in upwards of fifteen different pools at a time, sometimes using the same "sheet of integrity," sometimes with fifteen different sheets. So what is the best way to deal with multiple bracket entries? I'm sure there is a back-up power forward for Cal Tech who can make some complex algorithm that explains the perfect way to deal with the multiple bracket quandary. However, who has time for that schtuff? Personally, I don't like to participate with multiple brackets and haven't for years. But multiple bracket entries are a thing that commonly happens, and it only seems appropriate to address the issue, particularly at this stage of the tournament.

When it comes to using multiple brackets, my advice is to keep Bracketeering, that is, keep following the numbers. Don't simply spread out your picks so that you have as many chances as possible. What many people will do is pick four teams in their Final Four in one bracket, then fill out an additional bracket with four different teams. The logic? To have as many different teams in the Final Four in an effort to increase the odds of winning a pool. However, this logic is flawed, particularly in years where there are undeniably dominant teams that would be foolish to pick against, even if you are just trying to "increase the odds." When you are dealing with a tournament in which there are world-class teams, don't eschew picking them. Yet, if you have a group of teams remaining that are very close statistically and it's hard to pick between them, then maybe it is smart to spread your picks out. But if there are teams that you judge to be the best of the decade (or even just the best of that tournament), then go with the numbers and pick them over and over again, even if you are in two, ten, or six hundred different pools. The numbers really don't lie.

Rule 5.2: Have you ever heard of PPS? If not, it's a good acronym to learn, especially if you are struggling to break ties with your last few picks.

In the first few years of using my system, I never relied on PPS for anything. In fact, I didn't know a thing about it. There are way too many metrics worth considering to have PPS be the end-all, be-all of statistics. However, if you are having trouble trying to decide between two teams and all other methods that this book has discussed have proved inconclusive, let PPS try to guide you one way or the other.

So, what the heck is PPS anyways? No, it's not the Pirate Party of Switzerland, though they do use the same acronym. However, I doubt they could help you choose a matchup between West Virginia and Kentucky. PPS simply stands for Points Per Shot. That's all. A simple measure of how many points a team averages per shot attempt. Ultimately, this is a significant measure of a team's efficacy on offense, though it can be a tricky stat to use. For example, the team which led the nation in PPS in 2009-2010? The 19-13 Denver Pioneers of the Sun Belt Conference, of course. The problem with the Denver team was that as efficient as their offense was, they seldom shot the basketball, averaging less than 44 field goal attempts per game. But PPS can be one of those metrics that really exemplifies how successful a team can be come tournament time. In 2009-2010,

Butler was a respectable team that didn't have too many weaknesses, yet they really didn't demonstrate many overly dominant strengths as a squad. However, the Bulldogs ranked 8th in the nation in PPS, averaging 1.4 points for each shot attempt, which is impressive. Now granted, Butler wasn't a team that went wild shooting the ball, as they averaged just over 50 field goal attempts per game. Yet this stat shows just how efficient they were when the ball was in their hands. And how important can PPS be? Just imagine a team like Butler with a 1.4 PPS playing a team that has a PPS of less than 1.25. If each team takes a total of 60 shots per game, the team like Butler will score at least nine more points on average than its opponents. In more circumstances than not, teams are very close to one another in terms of PPS. And it's also very rare that teams take equal numbers of shot attempts, which is why stats like created-possession margin are absolutely critical to check. In tough call situations, however, PPS is a great statistic to glance at—and you can even benefit by looking at it in situations that don't seem like difficult calls, too, just to be safe.

Rule 5.3: If worse comes to worst, and you can't make a firm decision on your championship game picks, resort to third-tier techniques in order to come up with some sort of logical decision. Just don't make blind guesses or pick based on the strength of a school's engineering program. Those aren't logical decisions at all.

What do you do when all else fails, when everything from scoring margin to created-possession margin to free-throw percentage yields no real conclusive result? It's not often that these situations arise, but it's bound to happen at some point during the tournament, often at the end. Sure, this is an incredibly difficult position to be in, and for most people facing these kinds of tough decisions, the easiest solution appears to be flipping a coin. But I strongly advise against using tiebreakers that aren't founded on any sort of logic at all other than just dumb luck. (And trust me, it is dumb to flip a coin.) For me, when these types of situations arise, I utilize a few of what I call "third-tier tiebreakers." The three I use—and the order in which I use them—are (insert drumroll):

1) Head-to-head history: If it exists—and I mean within the past season, as it's pointless to look at the results of a 1951 matchup between two teams in the 2011 tournament—then head-to-head history between a pair of teams can give you at least some kind of idea of how they will play against one another.

2) Player and coaching experience: I typically hate to use this measure, since I think statistical performance is the best way to evaluate, well, anything. But if everything is completely gridlocked and there is no head-to-head history, then I prefer to give advantages to coaches who have a track record of success and teams composed of players who are in their junior and senior years. As with almost anything in life, additional experience does tend to provide at least a mild edge.

3) Normative evaluation of a team: That's a fancy and ever-so-schmancy way of saying that you can actually watch how a team plays (a simple internet search or a visit to a school's website should yield some kind of game film if you haven't already seen both teams play) and then decide through watching—rather than by using statistical analysis—which team's style of play is more conducive to success than the other's. (I know this is heresy to true stat-heads, but even they have to agree it is better than flipping a coin.)

Those are the three ways I break those seemingly deadlocked ties. You can either utilize one or all of these three methods or use your own creative license and come up with a method you think would be more effective. The point *I'm* trying to make is that under *no* circumstance should you be picking a winner blindly. There's just no place for that in Bracketeering.

ROUND SIX
Who Is Cutting Down the Net?

And here it is, the National Title Game. By now you should have whittled down your bracket to two teams that are nearly indistinguishable from one another and are squaring off in a contest that is far too close to call. Don't get me wrong: Some years there *is* that obvious pick. For example, it was hard to choose against the North Carolina Tar Heels in 2009. But chances are this will be the most difficult—and it's certainly the most important—decision of your bracket. So what do you do now that you're finally here? You are posed with the dilemma of picking between two teams that both could win the title, but only one will. How do you choose the winner? What I wanted to do with the last round is illustrate the decision-making process I use by looking at one of the closest championship games I can remember: the 2008 title game.

In my bracket, I correctly predicted that top-seeded Kansas would square off against top-seeded Memphis. But I was stuck. These were two of the most dominant teams in recent memory. Memphis was a high-powered squad led by future Number 1 overall pick Derrick Rose, while Kansas had a high number of future NBA draft picks on its roster, including Mario Chalmers, Brandon Rush, and Darrell Arthur. To give you an idea about how to make these kinds of seemingly impossible decisions, I am going to give you a walkthrough of how I evaluated the Kansas and Memphis game, and how I reached my final decision. My hope in doing this is to give you an idea of what statistics are most important and provide an overall understanding of how to break what appears to be an unbreakable tie. So without further ado, let's look at the round six decision-making process.

Step One: Look at scoring margin first. Always.

As the best metric of a team's overall talents on both offense and defense, you should always look at the scoring-margin difference between both teams that you are evaluating, whether the game is in the first round or in the last round or if you're trying to figure out who will win the 11-year-old division of a CYO basketball league. The Jayhawks entered the 2008 tournament with an NCAA-leading +19.9 scoring margin, an *unreasonably* high number that should have opened eyes everywhere. Surely this team should have clinched the title, and there was no reason to look at any more statistics, right? Not so fast. Memphis ranked *second* in the nation with an unbelievable +19.1 margin, meaning that the Jayhawks had an advantage of less than a single point in this basic stat. With these kind of matching numbers—as unreal as they were—no one had an advantage. However, scoring margin is the place we must always start.

Step Two: As soon as you finish looking at scoring margin, take a sip of your coffee. Then immediately look at created-possession margin.

In games like this, where the competition is so close to one another, even the smallest margin can go a long way. And guess what? Kansas and Memphis were both dominant in this statistic as well. Entering the tournament, the Jayhawks carried an otherworldly

+10.83 created-possession margin, only to be outdone—albeit very mildly—by the Tigers, who averaged 10.88 more created possessions per game than their opponents. Frankly, this is not too surprising, though it does make things a bit more difficult. Usually, I can make more than half my decisions about tournament games using these first two metrics. But Memphis and Kansas had made things a bit tricky. So what did we have so far? Well, Kansas had less than a point per game advantage over Memphis, and Memphis averaged less than 0.1 created possessions over Kansas. In other words, we really didn't have anything. But these are the first two steps we have to go through. And in this order.

Step Three: Is one team far more efficient with the basketball than the other? And remember, you must adjust a team's shooting percentages with their opponent's defensive averages. And vice. And versa.

As I displayed back in Round 3, it's important to look at how efficiently a team runs its offense, as having all the possessions in the world is worthless if you can't shoot a lick from the floor. And further, it's definitely important to factor in how potent an opponent's defensive game is, as that will certainly alter how effectively an offense performs. Going into the 2008 tournament, both Memphis and Kansas had top-flight offensive assaults, each ranking in the top 60 in the nation in field-goal percentage (Kansas was 3rd with an impressive 50.5 percent; Memphis was 55th with a respectable 46.6 percent). However, as spectacular as each team's offensive efficiency was, each of their impressive defensive attacks seemed primed to limit the other team's scoring capabilities. So what did I do? Adjust, of course. When factored in with Memphis' 6th-ranked defensive field-goal percentage, Kansas' jaw-dropping 50.5 percent from the field dropped to 44.4 percent. (Memphis' offense, when adjusted, sunk to 42.3 percent.) Now an extra two percentage points from the field wasn't going to be a clincher, but it was something certainly to put on the back burner of my mind: a slight advantage went to Kansas. Off to the next step.

Step Four: Keep Conference Factor in the back of your mind. Don't let it control your thinking process. Just know that it's there.

Conference Factor changes year to year, and in most years it's not too, too big of a deal, as championship matchups, most of the time, include teams from the so-called BCS conferences (Pac-10, SEC, ACC, Big East, Big 10, Big 12) that tend to always play very rigid competition. However, it is worth mentioning that Memphis played in Conference USA and wasn't facing the world's foremost collegiate powerhouses (sorry, Rice and Marshall). That's not to discredit everything that Memphis did, because the Tigers played half of their schedule out of conference, including games against some of the nation's top teams. However, some of their weaker in-conference games allowed Memphis to skew its stats—albeit slightly. Memphis was definitely worthy of being in the championship game, and was certainly capable of winning the whole shebang, but it was at least something to think about if those two teams ended up deadlocked statistically.

Step Five: Are there any foulers here? Remember, constant foul-ing—especially against teams that thrive from the line—can sway the outcome of a game.

Simply put: Kansas had 17.4 fouls per game, Memphis averaged 17.6. You had to be kidding me! So far, on paper at least, it seemed like the kind of game that could last forever, going into twenty over-times before becoming a contest that wasn't won by the better team statistically but rather by the squad with the fewest smokers and low-est cholesterol levels.

Step Six: Hmm, perhaps one of the teams relies heavily on the three-point shot, and perhaps the other team is effective at stop-ping it? Maybe? Maybe?

Eh, not so much here. Though Memphis had a higher reliance on the three-ball compared to Kansas (29.73 percent of its offense compared to 25.39 percent for Kansas), Memphis proved tougher defensively along the perimeter than Kansas, averaging nearly three percentage points better than the Jayhawks in terms of defensive three-point shooting percentage. Basically, this equates to a wash and neither team really had any sort of stark advantage over the other. Next.

Step Seven: Outstanding or dismal free-throw shooting can be a game-changing statistic. At least tell me we have something here.

And here I had finally found it. Until this point, Kansas had a razor-thin lead over the Tigers, so thin that you couldn't really even call it an advantage at all. But it turned out that their lead over Memphis was about to get a lot bigger. During the 2007-2008 regular season, Kansas averaged a respectably modest 70.2 percent from the free-throw line. Certainly Kansas could have done a bit better, having ranked 131st of 328 teams in the country going into the tournament, and their performance from the line was nothing to write home about—especially if you already lived at home. However, the 2007-2008 Memphis Tigers made the entire Kansas squad look as if they held doctoral degrees in free-throw making (I'm pretty sure the Ph.D. in free throws is offered by at least two SEC schools). Entering the 2008 tournament, the Memphis Tigers averaged a paltry 59.6 percent mark from the free-throw line. Look at that number again: 59.6 percent. Out of the 328 teams in Division I basketball that year, Memphis ranked 326th, just ahead of Winthrop (59.5 percent) and Washington (59.0). This kind of shooting percentage is a game breaker, and had the Tigers not been so overwhelmingly dominant in the other reaches of their game, a number like this could have made them a candidate to lose a Final Four or Elite Eight game— heck, even a second-round game. To put Memphis' numbers in perspective, if they were to get to the line ten times a game—a fairly standard amount—they would leave at least eight points a game on the board *on average.* That's unforgivable, and when a team is that mercurial from the line, it's no guarantee they will even reach that 60-ish percent mark.

It's important to note and red flag critical statistical issues like this, as they can decide who takes home the title. Before seeing this statistic, I was only slightly leaning towards Kansas because I *had* to pick *one* team to win the title. After this, barring a discovery of some crucial statistical disparities that I had yet to see, the Jayhawks were my pick to win the whole thing.

Step Eight: If Memphis and Kansas each had respectable free-throw percentages, then block differentials and PPS could be used to try to break ties. And if that doesn't work, it's time to use those "tertiary tiebreakers."

Had there not been the drastic free-throw percentage differential, I would have needed to rely on last-ditch tiebreakers to help figure out who would win that game. These included mostly block differentials and PPS. However, those wouldn't have been much help. To give an example: Memphis averaged 6.1 blocks per game going into the 2008 tournament. And Kansas? They averaged 6.2. Beyond that, in order to try and find some kind of logical tie-breaker, I would have resorted to what I consider the third-tier tiebreakers—head-to-head histories, player and coaching experience, and worse-case scenario, observation through game film. Thankfully, the Tigers made things a good deal easier for me with their dismal free-throw shooting.

As you can probably guess, I picked Kansas. And the winner of the 2008 National Title was…the Holy Cross Crusaders. I'm just kidding. It was Kansas, 75-68, in what was a rather close game. Kansas won the battle on the boards, Memphis had the edge with turnovers. The Jayhawks shot better from the field and ended up shooting over 93 percent from the free-throw line. And Memphis? Well, they managed just 63.2 percent from the charity stripe on 19 attempts, meaning that they left seven points on the board. Had the Tigers been a better shooting team from the line, the result of this game could have wound up very differently. But they had a very tragic flaw that was bound to get exposed, particularly in a close matchup against an extraordinarily talented team. So the moral of this story? Picking the national champion may end up being the most difficult choice in your bracket. But by following these steps, what once took a few days to research should only take 10-15 minutes tops. And the result should be worth it, too.

THE POST SCRIPT

For those of you who have read this and decided to use the Brack-eteering method, you might find yourself with a fewer hours of free time come the month of March. But by the time April rolls around, I hope you will be rather pleased with how your bracket turned out.

As I've stated time and time again, Bracketeering is by no means the blueprint to the perfect "sheet of integrity," that ever-so-elusive concept that has been dreamt and rumored about since the Mayan days. (Unfortunately, most Mayans also picked Gonzaga to win year after year.)

So when we're hunkered down in our own separate makeshift bunkers come the Madness in March, eating pizza for three meals a day while rooting against those schools that rejected us when we were high school seniors, just know that your buddy from the cu-bicle down the hall or that aunt you only see twice a year doesn't have the same advantage you do. Unless they've read this book. Of course.

AND THE ACKNOWLEDGMENTS

Hmm, who would I like to thank? Well firstly and mostly, I would like to thank a very supportive pair of amazing parents and two very wonderful and equally supportive sisters, Allisha and Michelle, for everything they have done for me throughout the years. I also want to thank my two grandparents, a great cast of friends, and some fantastic aunts and uncles (it sounds as if I'm building an ark, no?). I am very appreciative for a university staff member and a certain four undergraduate professors (you know your names) for helping shape me as a writer and person—especially Scott.

And lastly but not leastly, I owe a debt of gratitude that can never be repaid—not at the royalty rate they gave me, anyway—to Greg Pierce and the people of ACTA for encouraging me and letting me pen my first book. To all involved, I simply say, thank you.

Advance Praise for Bracketeering

It is so much fun to see the principles of sabermetrics being used to pick the NCAA Men's Basketball Tournament winner. I don't know if Andrew Clark's "system" works or not, but I'm sure going to try it when I fill out my brackets this year.

John Dewan, author of *Stat-of-the-Week* and
The Fielding Bible: Volumes I and II

Andrew Clark writes from a fan's perspective while offering expert advice. So spread everything out on the kitchen table, but don't make a pick until you read *Bracketeering*.

Larry Johnson, host of "Mustard and Johnson" on WEEI in Boston
and a former cartoonist for ESPN and *The Boston Globe*

Throw out the tea leaves; put down the darts. You're in good hands. Even a neophyte can make sense of picking brackets with Andrew Clark's clear and concise guidance. And even if you never intend to pick up a pencil or consult a computer, you'll still enjoy reading *Bracketeering*.

Bonnie Bryant, author of *The Saddle Club* series
and other books for young people